Scott the Astronaut

Tracy Kompelien

Consulting Editor, Diane Craig, M.A./Reading Specialist

Published by ABDO Publishing Company, 4940 Viking Drive, Edina, Minnesota 55435.

Copyright © 2005 by Abdo Consulting Group, Inc. International copyrights reserved in all countries. No part of this book may be reproduced in any form without written permission from the publisher. SandCastle™ is a trademark and logo of ABDO Publishing Company.

Printed in the United States.

Credits
Edited by: Pam Price
Curriculum Coordinator: Nancy Tuminelly
Cover and Interior Design and Production: Mighty Media
Photo and Illustration Credits: BananaStock Ltd., Comstock, Creatas, Hemera, ImageState, Tracy Kompelien, PhotoDisc, Stockbyte

Library of Congress Cataloging-in-Publication Data

Kompelien, Tracy, 1975-
  Scott the astronaut / Tracy Kompelien.
    p. cm. -- (Rhyme time)
  ISBN 1-59197-815-7 (hardcover)
  ISBN 1-59197-921-8 (paperback)
  1. English language--Rhyme--Juvenile literature. I. Title. II. Rhyme time (ABDO Publishing Company)

PE1517.K664 2004
428.1'3--dc22
2004049105

SandCastle™ books are created by a professional team of educators, reading specialists, and content developers around five essential components that include phonemic awareness, phonics, vocabulary, text comprehension, and fluency. All books are written, reviewed, and leveled for guided reading, early intervention reading, and Accelerated Reader® programs and designed for use in shared, guided, and independent reading and writing activities to support a balanced approach to literacy instruction.

Let Us Know

After reading the book, SandCastle would like you to tell us your stories about reading. What is your favorite page? Was there something hard that you needed help with? Share the ups and downs of learning to read. We want to hear from you! To get posted on the ABDO Publishing Company Web site, send us e-mail at:

sandcastle@abdopub.com

SandCastle Level: Fluent

Words that rhyme do not have to be spelled the same. These words rhyme with each other:

bought

pot

brought

sought

caught

spot

hot

thought

knot

trot

Allison has fun swimming with her dad when it is **hot**.

Mandy helps her mom carry the groceries they **bought**.

Robert's dad shows him how to tie a knot.

At the parade, everyone waved the flags that they **brought**.

Kimberly planted the daisies in a **pot**.

Tommy holds up the fish that he **caught**.

Cameron relaxes outside in his favorite spot.

Danielle and Janice went to the library to find the answers they **sought**.

Paige and Matthew **trot** across the beach with their parents.

Steven told his grandmother his idea and asked her what she **thought**.

Scott the Astronaut

Scott the astronaut wanted to explore the planet Trot.

Before his mission, he thought
he would bring some gear he bought.

Scott brought an apricot,

a rope to tie in a knot,

and a special pot that held a lot.

On his way out, he ran into a cosmonaut.

They became friends and talked a lot.

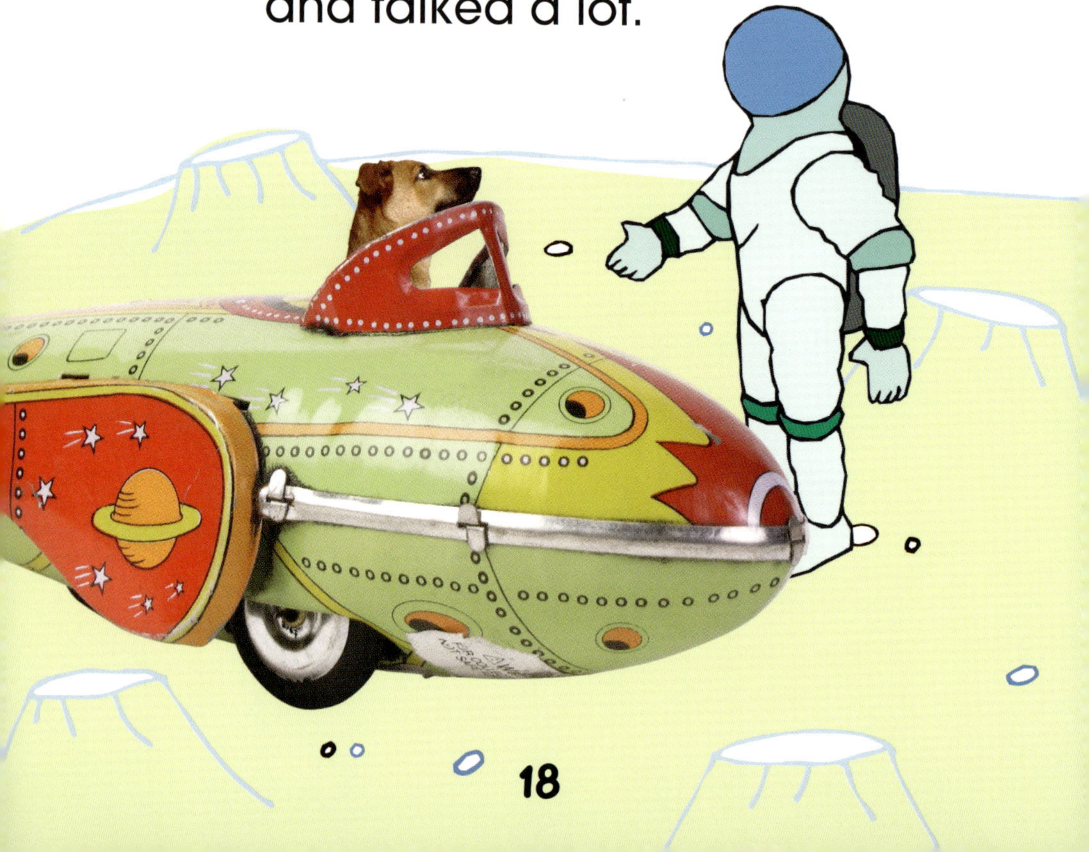

The next morning Scott felt hot.

He realized he had caught a fever from the cosmonaut.

So he tied the ice pack on with a knot.

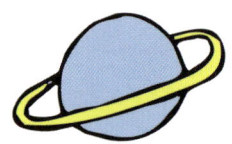

Scott made tea in his special pot and then ate his apricot.

Next he took a nap on his cot.

Scott's meal and nap hit the spot.
When he woke, he felt
as good as any astronaut.

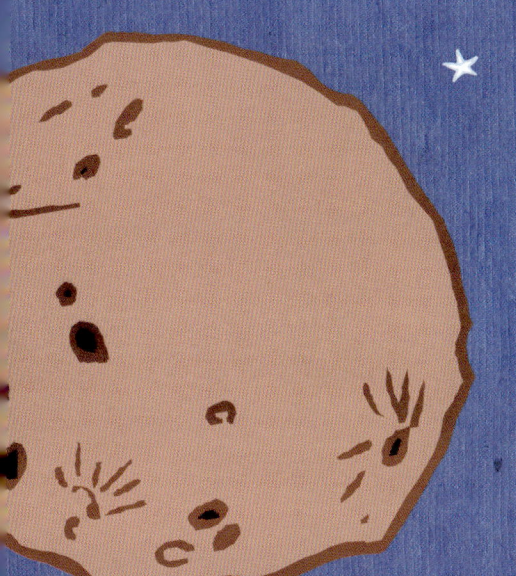

Now he was ready
to explore the planet Trot.

Rhyming Riddle

What do you call
a tangled rope stuck on a fishhook?

Caught knot

Glossary

apricot. an oval, orange-colored fruit related to the peach

astronaut. a person who is trained to travel in space

cosmonaut. an astronaut from Russia

cot. a small bed that can be folded up

seek. to search or look for

sought. past tense of seek

trot. to ride a horse that is running at a moderately fast pace

About SandCastle™

A professional team of educators, reading specialists, and content developers created the SandCastle™ series to support young readers as they develop reading skills and strategies and increase their general knowledge. The SandCastle™ series has four levels that correspond to early literacy development in young children. The levels are provided to help teachers and parents select the appropriate books for young readers.

Emerging Readers
(no flags)

Beginning Readers
(1 flag)

Transitional Readers
(2 flags)

Fluent Readers
(3 flags)

These levels are meant only as a guide. All levels are subject to change.

To see a complete list of SandCastle™ books and other nonfiction titles from ABDO Publishing Company, visit **www.abdopub.com** or contact us at:
4940 Viking Drive, Edina, Minnesota 55435 • 1-800-800-1312 • fax: 1-952-831-1632